MACHINE MAGIC!

Machines are truly magical because they can transform the smallest pushes or pulls into the greatest forces. We use them to lift heavy loads, to transport things and to perform tasks at very high speeds. Consisting of pulleys and levers, and other contraptions, machines are often driven by basic substances such as water and air. The audience will be stunned by your unbelievable powers as water is made to travel uphill and cylinders creep up pieces of string. You are sure to generate lots of excitement!

BE AN EXPERT MAGICIAN

PREPARING YOUR ROUTINE

There is much more to being a magician than just doing tricks. It is important that you and your assistant practise your whole routine lots of times, so that your performance goes smoothly when you do it for real. You will be a more entertaining magician if you do.

PROPS

Props are all the bits and pieces of equipment that a magician uses during an act. These include your clothes as well as the tricks themselves. It's a good idea to make a magician's trunk from a large box to keep all your props in. During your routine, you can dip into the trunk, pulling out all sorts of equipment and crazy objects (see Distraction). You could tell jokes about these objects.

PROPS LIST

Magic wand	Glass jars
Top hat	Bowl
Waistcoat	String
Bow tie	Paints
Silk scarves	Elastic
Cardboard	Coloured paper
Corrugated card	Sticky tape
Wooden rod or	Square of cloth
garden stick	Plastic tubing	Scissors
Balloons	Glue	Waterproof
	Straws	sealant

WHICH TRICKS?

Work out which tricks you want to put in your routine. Put in some long tricks and some short tricks. This will keep your audience interested.

If you can, include a trick that you can keep going back to during the routine. Magicians call this a "running gag".

MAGICIAN'S PATTER

Patter is what you say during your routine. Good patter makes a routine much more interesting and allows it to

run much more smoothly. It is a good way to entertain your audience during the slower parts of your routine. Try to make up a story for each trick, and remember to thank your audience at the end. Practise your patter when you practise your tricks.

DISTRACTION

Distraction is an important part of a magician's routine. By waving a colourful scarf in the air or telling a joke, you can take an audience's attention away from something you'd rather they didn't see!

KEEP IT SECRET

The best magicians never give away their secrets. If anyone asks how your tricks work, just reply, "By magic!" Then you can impress people with your tricks again and again.

INTRODUCING MAGIC MARIA
AND THE
DOWN THE TRAP TRICK

Magic Maria has a mysterious box which makes things disappear without trace!

Ask for a volunteer from the audience. Show your volunteer that the box is empty, and ask him or her to place a straw inside the box. Tap the box with your wand and secretly operate the trap door. Then show the empty box.

WHAT YOU NEED
Cardboard box, Glue
Thin wooden rod, Paints
Elastic, Stiff card, Straws

THE SCIENCE
BEHIND THE TRICK

The trap door is opened by a system of levers. Putting the box down pushes the bottom of the lever up. The top end of the lever is pulled down, taking the front of the trap door with it. An upward force is turned into a downward force.

Trap door

Lever

1 Cut off the top and bottom of a cardboard box. Cut out a triangle in the sides to make the front slope down (a). Fit in a piece of card with tabs (b), 5cm above the bottom. Tie a piece of elastic through a pierced hole at one end. Push a wooden rod underneath the card to support it. Glue a strip of card in the back of the box for the rear edge of the trap door to rest on (c).

2 Add two more wooden rods stuck together at right angles. Tape one end to the underneath of the trap door (d). Cut a slot and hole in the bottom of the box. The rod should stick through the slot. Push the elastic through the hole and tie it to keep the door just shut (e).

(a)

(b)

(c)

(d)

(e)

WHAT YOU NEED
String
Cardboard tube
Thin wooden rods
Plastic tube
Card
Sticky tape

INTRODUCING MAGIC MARTIN
AND THE
SPOOKY CYLINDER TRICK

It's really spooky! Under Magic Martin's command the cylinder rises up the string!

Ask the audience to watch the cylinder carefully as you stretch out a piece of string with both hands. Pull on both ends of the string and the cylinder will seem to rise up the string.

THE SCIENCE BEHIND THE TRICK

The string and the rod form a pulley system. Pulling the strings apart lifts the cylinder. The greater the number of turns of string, the easier it is to lift the cylinder, but the further you have to pull.

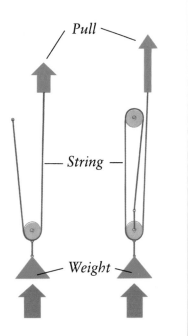

Pull

String

Weight

1 Cut a piece of wooden rod just long enough to jam inside the cylinder. Slide a short piece of plastic tube over the top. Wind round pieces of tape, which will keep the string in place.

2 Tie a loop in the end of a piece of string. Tie a second piece of string to the loop, and thread it over the rod, back through the loop and out of the bottom of the cylinder. The first string goes out of the top of the cylinder.

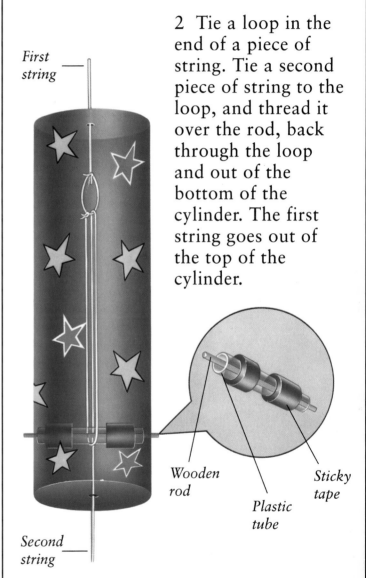

First string

Second string

Wooden rod

Plastic tube

Sticky tape

3 Cut two circles of card to fit over the ends of the cylinder. Pierce a hole in each one, thread the strings through and glue them to the ends of the cylinder.

INTRODUCING MAGIC MARIA
AND THE
WEIRD GEARS TRICK

It's really weird! The wheels turn at the same speed even when the gears are changed!

Begin by asking for a volunteer from your audience. Ask him or her to look into the box. Then ask whether he or she thinks that the big gear or the small gear will make the pointer wheel turn faster. They will probably say the big gear. Turn the handle with one gear in place and then the other. Amazingly the pointer wheel will turn at the same speed each time.

WHAT YOU NEED
Corrugated card
Stiff card
Cardboard tubes
Glue
Cardboard box
Thin wooden rod

THE SCIENCE BEHIND THE TRICK

When one gear wheel turns another, the number of turns the second one makes depends on the number of teeth on each gear wheel, not their size. Although the centre gears turn different amounts because they are different sizes, they make the pointer wheel turn the same amount.

Large centre gear

Small centre gear

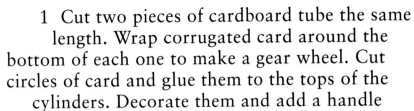

1 Cut two pieces of cardboard tube the same length. Wrap corrugated card around the bottom of each one to make a gear wheel. Cut circles of card and glue them to the tops of the cylinders. Decorate them and add a handle made of rod to one and an arrow to the other (a). Now cut two shorter lengths of tube. Cut them along the side and overlap the edges to make thinner tubes which fit neatly inside the gear tubes. Glue these to the base of a cardboard box so that the edges of the gear wheels touch (b).

(a)

(b)

(c)　　　　(d)

2 Make two more gear wheels, one from the same tube as before and another from a larger tube so that it has more teeth. Glue circles of card to the tops and bottoms and make holes in them (c). Mount the gears in a cardboard frame as shown, using wood rods for axles (d).

INTRODUCING MAGIC MIRANDA
AND THE
MAGIC GRAB TRICK

Only Magic Miranda can use the magic grab to pick things up. It won't work for anybody else!

For this trick you need a volunteer. Ask your volunteer to watch as you pick up an object with the grab (remember to hold the end with the balloon in it). Let your volunteer have a try. As you hand over the grab, turn it round so that he or she is holding the end with the rod in it. Picking up the object will now be impossible.

WHAT YOU NEED
Thick strips of card
Thick wooden rod
Balloon
Sticky tape
Coloured paper

THE SCIENCE BEHIND THE TRICK

The grab does not work at one end because you cannot push the sides together. But if the balloon end is squeezed, air is compressed and the card comes together. It forms a lever, similar to a pair of tweezers.

Push

Push

GETTING PREPARED

1 Cut a piece of wooden rod the same width as your two strips of card. Blow some air into a balloon and tie the neck. Attach both between the strips of card.

Card

Balloon

Wooden rod

2 Stick coloured paper around the grab to hide the rod and balloon.

Coloured paper

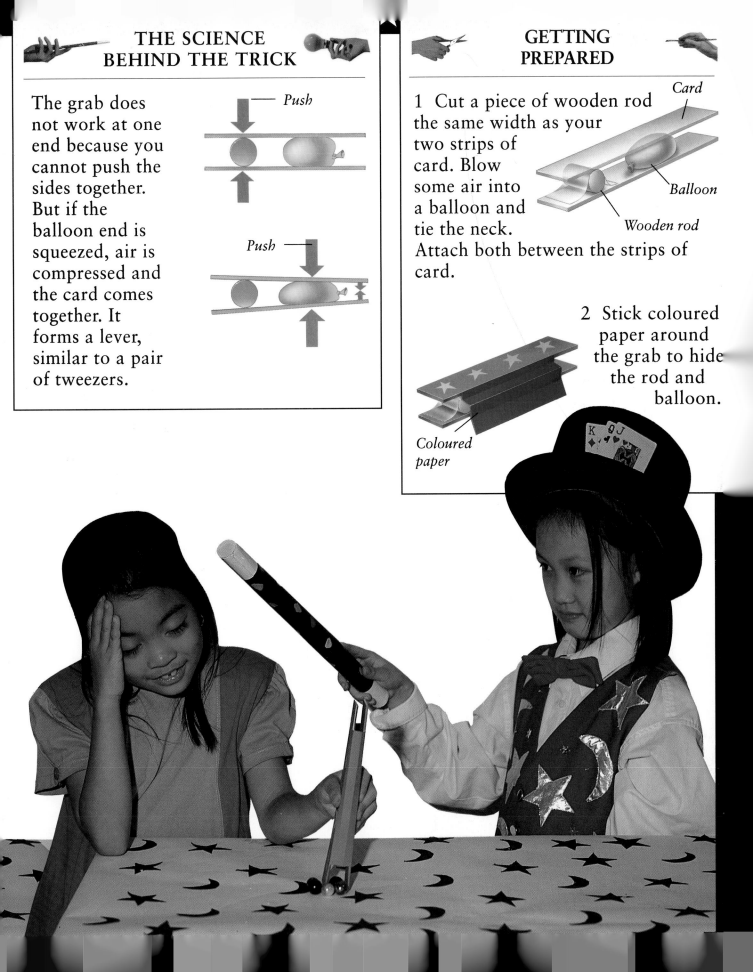

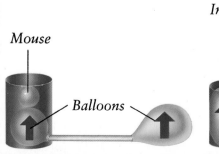

INTRODUCING MAGIC MARIA
— AND THE —
MAGICAL MOUSE

The audience is stunned as Magic Maria makes the magical mouse rise out of its hole!

This trick is a good opportunity for some magician's patter. You could tell your audience that the mouse is very shy and will only come out of its hole if they shout very loudly. Ask your audience to shout to coax the mouse out. Gradually press on the hidden balloon and the mouse will rise.

WHAT YOU NEED
Plastic tubing
Balloons
Cardboard box
Elastic bands
Card
Sticky tape

THE SCIENCE
BEHIND THE TRICK

The plastic tubing and the balloons form a kind of machine. Pressing one balloon makes the other inflate, pushing the mouse upwards. Many complicated machines use compressed air in this way to make their parts move. Machines that use air like this are called pneumatic machines.

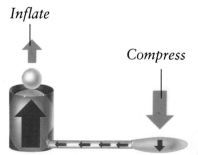

Mouse

Balloons

Inflate

Compress

Mouse

Paper cylinder

Balloon

Cardboard box

1 Cut two holes in a cardboard box, one in the back and one in the top. Push a length of plastic tubing through the holes.

2 Put a balloon over one end of the tube. Blow up another balloon and put it over the other end of the tube. Hold the balloon necks in place with elastic bands.

Plastic tubing

Balloon

3 Cut out and decorate a mouse shape and attach it with tape to the balloon on the top of the box. Make a paper cylinder to hide this balloon and attach it to the top of the box as well.

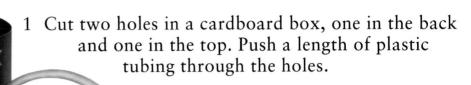

INTRODUCING MAGIC MIRANDA
AND THE
BARMY BALANCE TRICK

It doesn't matter which weights Magic Miranda puts on it, the barmy balance balances every time!

Start the trick with no weights on the barmy balance. Put a large jar on the left-hand end (left-hand as you look at the balance). Now put another large jar on the right-hand end. The bar will balance. Take away the jars. Put the small jar on the left-hand end and then a large jar on the right-hand end. Incredibly, the bar will balance again.

WHAT YOU NEED
Jars with lids (large and small)
Plank of wood
Wooden rods
Stiff card
Coloured paper

THE SCIENCE BEHIND THE TRICK

The barmy balance is a simple lever. Two weights at equal distance along make it balance. But the further the

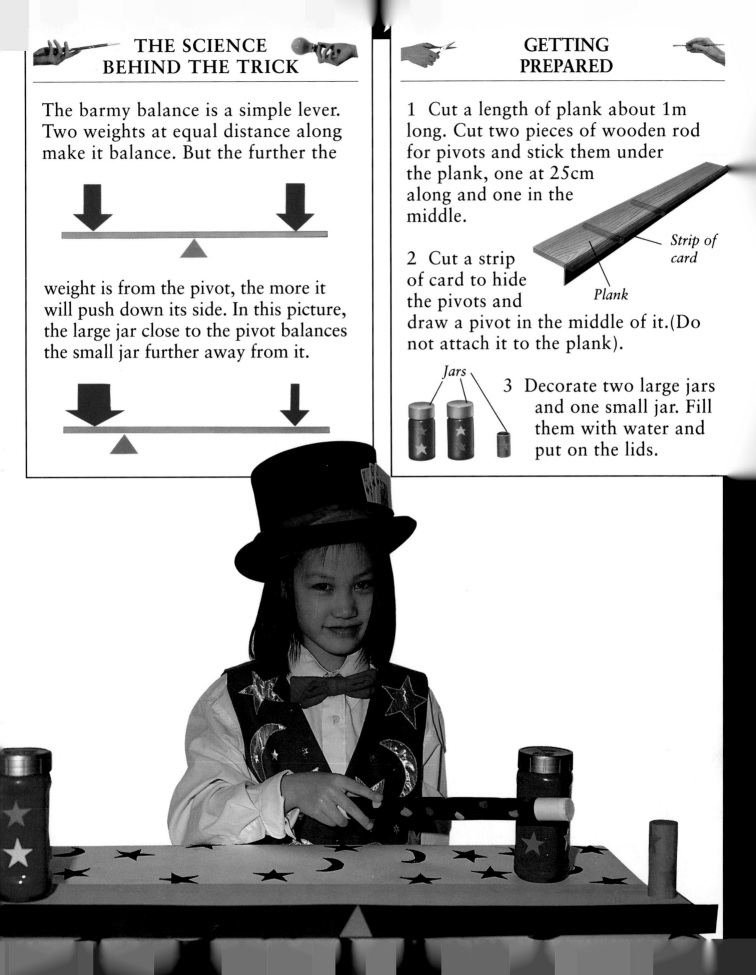

weight is from the pivot, the more it will push down its side. In this picture, the large jar close to the pivot balances the small jar further away from it.

GETTING PREPARED

1 Cut a length of plank about 1m long. Cut two pieces of wooden rod for pivots and stick them under the plank, one at 25cm along and one in the middle.

Strip of card

Plank

2 Cut a strip of card to hide the pivots and draw a pivot in the middle of it.(Do not attach it to the plank).

Jars

3 Decorate two large jars and one small jar. Fill them with water and put on the lids.

INTRODUCING MAGIC MANDY
AND THE
MAGIC TUBE TRICK

Surely it's impossible! Can Magic Mandy really make water flow uphill?

Start the trick with the bowl of water and the empty container in position on your table. Announce that you can make the water flow uphill from the bowl to the container. Now bring out the magic tube. Dip one end into the water and hold the other end over the container. Gradually turn the tube and after a few moments water will begin to pour into the container.

WHAT YOU NEED
Plastic tubing (about 1cm in diameter)
Cardboard tube
Card
Waterproof paints
Waterproof sticky tape
Bowl

THE SCIENCE BEHIND THE TRICK

The magic tube is a small form of a machine called an Archimedean screw. It lifts the water to a higher level as you turn the tube. These screws are used to raise water uphill for crops.

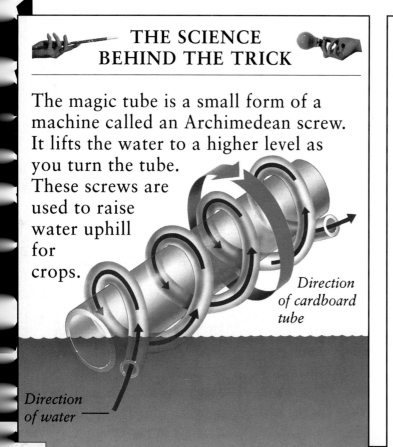

Direction of cardboard tube

Direction of water

GETTING PREPARED

1 Cover the ends of a cardboard tube with sticky tape.
Wrap a length of plastic tubing around the cylinder as shown, fixing it in place with sticky tape.

Plastic tubing

Cardboard tube

2 Wrap a piece of card around the outside to cover the tubing. Paint the outside with waterproof paints to look like a magic wand.

Painted card

INTRODUCING MAGIC MIRANDA
AND THE
SURPRISING STATUE TRICK

Magic Miranda uses her powers to make the statue rise mysteriously out of the box!

Start with the two boxes on your table. The plastic tubing should be hidden away behind. Tell your audience that there is a magic statue inside one of the boxes. Ask them to shout some magic words to make it come out. Wave your wand over the box and carefully press the other box. The statue will rise as if by magic!

WHAT YOU NEED
Balloons
Plastic tubing
Plastic drinks bottles
Cardboard boxes
Plastic cup
Waterproof sealant
Stiff card

THE SCIENCE BEHIND THE TRICK

This is called a hydraulic machine because it uses the force of water to make the parts move.

This trick works because the balloon pushes water down the tube into the other container, lifting the weight.

Pressure

Lift

GETTING PREPARED

1 Cut off the bottoms of two plastic drinks bottles. Pierce a hole in each one and push the ends of a piece of plastic tubing into the holes. Seal the ends with waterproof sealant. Cover each container with a cardboard box.

Plastic bottle   Balloon   Card   Statue

Holes

2 Push a blown-up balloon into one container and put a lid on its box. Make a statue from card and stick it on top of some more stiff card. Cut a hole in the box lid and glue a bottomless plastic cup under it to guide the statue. Finally, pour water into the containers.

INTRODUCING MAGIC MANDY
AND THE
SUPERSTRONG MAGICIAN

Magic Mandy gives herself super human powers. Now she's stronger than two people!

Wave your magic wand about and pretend to cast a spell on yourself. Ask for two volunteers from your audience. Ask each of them to hold a pole (they should put one hand at each end). Hold the loose end of the string yourself. Now tell them to try to pull the poles apart. Pull on the string yourself and your volunteers will be pulled together!

WHAT YOU NEED
Thick wooden poles or broomsticks
Thick string
Sticky tape

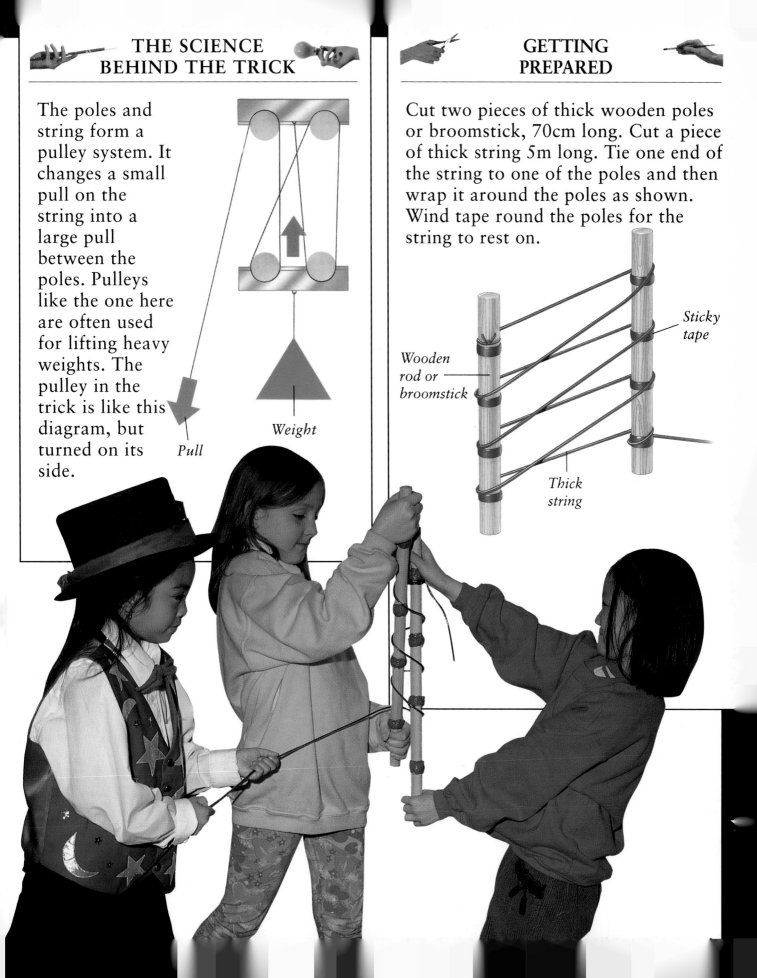

THE SCIENCE BEHIND THE TRICK

The poles and string form a pulley system. It changes a small pull on the string into a large pull between the poles. Pulleys like the one here are often used for lifting heavy weights. The pulley in the trick is like this diagram, but turned on its side.

Weight

Pull

GETTING PREPARED

Cut two pieces of thick wooden poles or broomstick, 70cm long. Cut a piece of thick string 5m long. Tie one end of the string to one of the poles and then wrap it around the poles as shown. Wind tape round the poles for the string to rest on.

Sticky tape

Wooden rod or broomstick

Thick string

INTRODUCING MAGIC MARTIN
AND THE
RISING PUPPET TRICK

As if by magic the puppet appears from behind the curtain. And then it's gone!

Start the trick with the curtain laid on your table. The puppet and strings should be hidden under it. Pick up the curtain by the corners, gripping the strings as well. Pull the strings gently and the puppet will rise mysteriously above the curtain.

WHAT YOU NEED
Square of cloth
String
Thick card
Coloured pens or paints

THE SCIENCE BEHIND THE TRICK

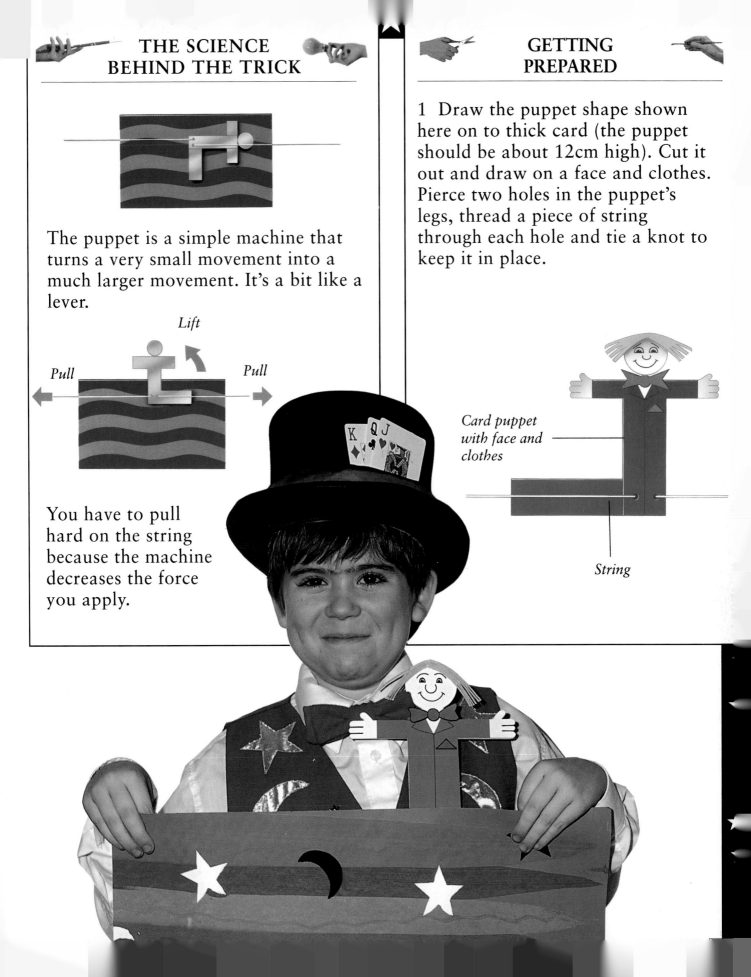

The puppet is a simple machine that turns a very small movement into a much larger movement. It's a bit like a lever.

Lift

Pull   *Pull*

You have to pull hard on the string because the machine decreases the force you apply.

GETTING PREPARED

1 Draw the puppet shape shown here on to thick card (the puppet should be about 12cm high). Cut it out and draw on a face and clothes. Pierce two holes in the puppet's legs, thread a piece of string through each hole and tie a knot to keep it in place.

Card puppet with face and clothes

String

HINTS AND TIPS

Here are some hints and tips for making your props. Good props will make your act look more professional. So spend time making and decorating your props, and look after them carefully. As well as the special props you need for each trick, try to make some general props such as a waistcoat and magic wand.

Decorate your props with magic shapes cut from coloured paper. Paint bottles and tubes with oil-based paint.

You will need sticky tape and glue to make props. Double-sided tape might also be useful. Thick fabric-based tape is good for joining the edges of boxes together, and it's easy to paint too.

Stencilling is a good way to decorate large areas. Cut magic shapes such as stars and crescent moons out of card. Throw away the shape, but keep the hole! Put the hole over your surface and paint through it with a sponge.

Your act will look extra professional if you make a proper stage set. This is easy if you have a backcloth to hang behind the stage. A large piece of black material is most effective. Using silver paint, stencil on stars and moons. Also decorate pieces of cloth to throw over your table. The overall atmosphere should be one of mystery and magic.

Make your own magician's clothes. Try to find an old hat and waistcoat to decorate. If you can find some silvery material, cut out stars and moons and sew them on. An alternative is to use sequins, or anything else that is shiny and dramatic.

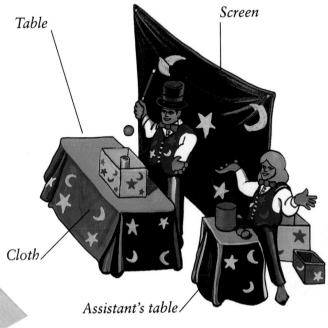

Table

Screen

Cloth

Assistant's table

Make a magician's table by draping a cloth over an ordinary table. Put props out of sight underneath.

GLOSSARY

GEARS A combination of cog wheels which transfer motion from large to small wheels, or more generally, any system of parts which produce motion.

HYDRAULIC MACHINES These are powered by water or other liquids, pushed through pipes or channels. Pressure from the liquid can either transfer or generate power.

LEVERS These are rigid bars supported or pivoted at some point along their length. Pressure applied at one point on the bar can move a load from another point.

MACHINE Any instrument which converts motion.

PIVOT The position from which an object turns. Axles are a type of pivot.

PNEUMATIC MACHINES These are powered by compressed air (air molecules squeezed together into a small space). Air pushes against a piston which then pushes against a device such as a hammer.

PULLEY SYSTEMS Use wheels with cord passing over them to change the direction of power or increase speed.

INDEX